The Chinese Fortune-Telling System

BaZi Method

By G L Golding

No part of this book may be copied, used, subsumed, or exploited in fact, field of thought or general idea, by any other authors or persons, or to be stored in a retrieval system, transmitted or reproduced in any way, including but not limited to digital copying and printing in any form whatsoever worldwide without the prior agreement and written permission of the author.

For substantial discounts on bulk quantities of this book, please email to: **goldingbook@gmail.com**

Published by

Good Port

Copyright © 2012 G L Golding
Edited by CreateSpace Editing Services
All rights reserved.
ISBN-13:978-981-07-3607-1
EBook: 978-981-07-3608-8

DEDICATION

This book will allow you to acquire the mystery of the Chinese fortune-telling system that has always been secretly and mysteriously related to people's destiny and life.

Table of Contents

This page is intended to be blank.

INTRODUCTION

When we talk about fortune-telling,

people usually classify it as a divine or superstitious idea. For those who have not studied the Chinese Fortune-telling system in depth, perhaps this is the case. But today, many scientists and philosophers accept the possibility of the existence on a predetermined or "mapped" individual life path— fate in advance. Researchers are now about to prove that the relationships between our fate are defined by nature, that is, a combination of the time, day, and year of our birth. And most importantly, by

studying the BaZi method, one of the most historically proven Chinese fortune-telling systems, you will soon be able to understand and realize that the practice is not a form of superstition. Learning the principles and logic of the system could be a key for you to unlock your inner potential and to decode your life. This book will allow you to acquire the mystery of the Chinese fortune-telling system that has always been secretly and mysteriously related to people's destiny and life.

In life, we are consistently in doubt and often encounter times when things seem to go wrong and there is nothing we can do about it. There are a few main reasons that people seek fortune-telling: because they are lost, indecisive, conflicted, or wonder about what lies ahead of them. We always hear about people saying success depends on your luck. Even the famous Donald Trump said, "Everything in life is luck." Luck is the ingredient of someone's success. So this will lead us to the question:

Do I have the luck?

We all know that luck, be it good or bad, occurs beyond one's control, without regard to one's will, intention, or desired result. The partial reason that fortune-telling has become most popular is because many people want to know their fate. Indeed in the concept of Chinese fortune-telling, there is a belief that our life is predetermined and we all have our own destiny. Everyone comes to this world with a purpose, we are all unique in our own ways, and everyone is better at certain things than others. Some people come for fortune-telling because they feel a sense of

uncertainty or insecurity or are perhaps unsatisfied with their present situation. The right attitude of seeking answers about your life is to accept that:

1. All things come with good or bad. Nobody will have a perfect life. Even most of the rich and famous people we hear about have suffered when they were young.

2. When we change our heart and thoughts, we change everything.

3. Outstanding is good, but being ordinary is great.

This page is intended to be blank.

THE CHINESE FORTUNE-TELLING PRACTICE

According to Wikipedia, Chinese fortune-telling is the practice of predicting, interpreting, and understanding a person's life. For many years, there were a few misconceptions of Chinese fortune-telling. It was known as a form of superstition, a type of religion that was unsustainable because it usually invoked deities or spirits. The study of the ancient Chinese fortune-telling system of BaZi, however, is a process of gathering one person's information and further analyzing it to form a detailed report of that person based on the day, time, and year that he was

born. Using a specific formula, it provides information about a person's personality, interests, abilities, career, and wealth. For a master who practiced Chinese fortune-telling back many years ago in China, it is a form of science taught from the oldest beliefs of their ancestors. During that time, many emperors in China recruited the best masters to help them make special decisions. Historically, the components that make up those life studies involve I Ching, which deals with the five elements, the outcome of sun and earth, known as horoscopes.

Recently, BaZi and I Ching have been adopted as methods of fortune-telling. It started to draw attention to the world, including the Western countries. Nevertheless, the practice of fortune-telling is not an outdated custom It is a way for many traditional Asian families to continue with their beliefs. It has indeed proven that the popularity of fortune-telling has spread widely not only within China but also Japan, India, and many countries. In this book, we are going to learn about BaZi, derived from the influence of I Ching, a method of interpreting a person's life, fate, and

fortune.

RELATIONSHIP BETWEEN BAZI AND SCIENCE

BaZi (also known as the Four Pillars of Destiny) was taught by Xú ZiPíng (徐子平) from The Scholarly School begun during the Song dynasty. It emphasizes interpreting our life journey by code, a secret code that each of us owns. It is believed that everyone has their own code from the day they are born, a birth code that they belong to. And these codes could help you understand the relationship between your ability, interests, and paths that you choose. Many researchers further consider that luck or destiny is also deeply affected by

the environment, place, and people we encountered in our life. When two persons share the same birth day, they might have a different life or circumstance due to the environment and people surrounding them. This is why each of us has our own life, making us all unique. We cannot assume that the same birthday will have the same fate, luck, or life.

So why do we bother to find out?

According to the book of Tao, the code of your life is the key to your life. Finding out your BaZi life chart could help you understand your inner strength and weakness. Having the key of your life could allow you to release that inner strength so that you might know and utilize it. At the same time, you could also change the ways to make things work for a better outcome.

So is interpreting life's code a superstitious approach? As the great Tao master said, "A great man should know his life, but not be mastered by his fate." So, there is really no harm knowing one's fate. But he should learn not to just listen to what was told and allow fate to manipulate. The philosophy and idea is to always try your best, and the results are up to heaven (or the God that you believe in) to decide.

DIFFERENCES OF BAZI TEACHING

BaZi, in Chinese, is translated as Eight Characters; it also has another name known as The Four Pillars of Destiny. Although there are only eight characters in a BaZi chart, the character of the relationship is complex because it integrates with the combination of the yin and yang, the Five Elements, and Lunar mathematical theory. It has been regarded as China's important traditional astrology.

There are many schools that carry out the studies of BaZi; each has its own method of interpreting it. But for all means of practices, the BaZi basic theory includes yin and yang, the Lunar, horoscopes, numerology, etc.

The ancient theories of the BaZi and elements has spread widely since the olden days. Researchers and followers today continue to investigate and study the ancient theories. In fact, there are no unified understandings since the old theories have been passed on with many changes and improvisation, which have resulted in a large variety of theories available. This has made it extremely difficult to learn and has also, in some way, contributed to the failure and accuracy of the prediction.

Let's get started!

THE BAZI AS THE FOUR PILLARS OF DESTINY

The Chinese, in ancient times, used information obtained from a person's BaZi to find symbols and direction for their future undertakings and decision making. The emperors of many dynasties hired the most skillful masters to help them predict things. Commoners used BaZi and feng shui to learn how to improve their lives. They created a model of human quality of life that depends on three main factors: Heaven Luck, Earth Luck, and Man Luck.

The three main factors are determined in the following ways:

Heaven Luck – The Heaven Luck is your pre-destined plan that heaven has for you. This is an uncontrollable factor.

Earth Luck – The Earth Luck is the place that you are born, which impacts your life and decisions you make. You can change it by applying feng shui or sometimes by moving to a new environment.

Man Luck – The Man Luck is the aspect of your work, education, and relationships. At some point you get to decide the things you want, and all of these decisions will impact your life.

BaZi, or the Four Pillars of Destiny, is a Chinese conceptual term that describes the four components creating a person's fate or destiny. You can consider this as a map of one life journey. Be it good or bad, people do not have a choice about the path that was given to them. The four components within the moment of birth are year, month, day, and time (hour). Because the four pillars is so relevant, the concept is also used as a form of component for other methods of fortune-telling practices, such as zi wei dou shu (紫微斗数) within the

realm of Chinese astrology.

First we introduce the concept of The Five Elements and The Eight Characters that are used to interpret one's life and fate.

The Five Elements, also known as Wu Xing (五行), consists of:

Element	Chinese	Pinyin
Wood	木	Mu
Fire	火	Huo
Earth	土	Tu
Metal	金	Jin
Water	水	Shui

Fig 1.1

The Five Elements is an ancient Chinese concept that is widely used in philosophy and Chinese medicine. It's the relationship between nature and the rise and fall of the Five Elements. Nature changes not only affect the fate of the people but also make everything in the universe loop endlessly.

INTERPRETATION OF ELEMENTS COMBINATION

The Interactions of Wu Xing (Fig 1.2):
The blue arrows represent the creation cycle, and the black arrows represent an overcoming cycle.

Fig 1.2

The principle of five phases describes two cycles of interactions between the phases: a generating or creation cycle, known as "mother-son," and an overcoming or destruction cycle, known as "grandfather-nephew."

Generating

The five elements are usually used to describe the state in nature:

Wood/Spring: a period of growth, which generates abundant wood and vitality.

Fire/Summer: a period of heat, which supports the fire and energy.

Metal/Autumn: a period of fruition, which harvests crops and bears fruit.

Water/Winter: a period of retreat, where things are silent and still.

Generate/Create (this cycle might also be called "beget" or "engender.")

> Wood feeds Fire;
>
> Fire creates Earth (ash);
>
> Earth bears Metal;
>
> Metal carries Water (as in a bucket or tap, or water condenses on metal);
>
> Water nourishes Wood.

Destruct/Overcome (This cycle might also be called "control" or "restrain.")

Wood parts Earth (such as roots; or trees can prevent soil erosion);

Metal chops Wood;

Fire melts Metal;

Water quenches Fire;

Earth dams (or muddies or absorbs) Water.

Refer to Figure 1.2, which reflects the relationship between different elements.

Five Elements Generate:

Gold →Water

Water → Wood

Wood → Fire

Fire → Soil

Soil → Gold.

Five Elements Destruct:

Metal >< Wood

Wood >< Earth

Earth >< Water

Water >< Fire

Fire >< Metal.

To understand how the BaZi is being structured, we first need to follow a formula and arrangement for each of the characters in a specific format. The format of BaZi is structured with 4 Heavenly Stems and 4 Earthly Branches. We will examine each of these in later chapters. To arrange your life palm, or BaZi, you will also need a Chinese Thousand Years calendar. You will refer to this tool for the dates of the elements you belong to according to the specific day that you were born. Alternatively, I have created online software that aims to help readers arrange their BaZi. Feel

free to try it out! As a beginner, relying on a computer is not a bad idea for a quick start. Ultimately, it is the objective of this book to help readers understand the basic structure and concept of BaZi and how it is accountable when used with the historical books and information passed down by our ancestors.

THE BAZI STRUCTURE

If you have never learned the eight characters, or BaZi, it is essential that you must first understand the five elements nature. You will notice as soon as you start to plot your BaZi that each element has a relationship with all the others. We use the outcome of these combinations to interpret how it impacts our lives.

First we start with the easiest way to render the character of the heavenly stems and to understand the interactive relationship of the Five Elements represented to each word in the Earthly Branches.

Hour 時	Day Master 日主	Month 月	Year 年	Ten Years 大運	Current Year 小運
Your Child	Yourself	Parents	Grand-parents		
	Spouse				

Fig 2.1

These columns represent:

1. The Hour that we were born

2. The Day that you were born

3. The Month that you were born

4. The Year that you were born

5. The Ten Years Period, which provides information about your ten years luck indicator

6. The Current Year Period, which provides information about your year luck indicator for a particular year

Each of the pillars also represents the relationships between your grandparents, parents, spouse, and your child. In brief, the BaZi obtains all the information that actually derives from us.

Completed BaZi Chart

A complete BaZi consists of the following:

> 1. The eight characters (八字) of BaZi or Four Pillars of Destiny.

> 2. Early childhood luck period or "Tong xian" (童限).

> 3. Decade (10 years) luck period or "Ta Yun" (大運) luck.

> 4. The yearly luck.

The BaZi, or Chinese Four Pillars of Destiny, is a branch of study of Chinese metaphysical science. The Four Pillars Chart is derived from the date of birth of a person using the Chinese Lunar-Solar Calendar. By formulating the BaZi chart, we can use it to study the characteristics of an individual and their fate and luck. The relationships interact between the individual and the surrounding environment.

Within a BaZi Chart, the Day Master is considered the most important element, which represents yourself. The quality of the Day Master will determine (by year or each ten years) the outcome of your fate and luck. And the people who have the same cycle of the luck for Strong Day Master versus a Weak Day Master are totally the opposite.

The Ten Years Cycle (大運)

This represents the luck period of an individual. It changes every ten years. By using the BaZi's ten years luck cycle, we could further interpret and analyze an individual's future luck of each period of ten years or more. A person's BaZi chart includes a reading of his/her Health, Wealth, and Relationship. The ten years luck cycle can be good or bad depending on its relationship (destroy or embrace) with the Day Master.

The Four Pillars chart can also forecast the strength and weakness in our destiny, which represents the ups and downs of life, by comparing the interaction of the Four Pillars chart with the Ten-Year Luck Pillars.

Knowing the elementsStem and Branch (天干地支)

The above four characters in the chart are the Stem (天干), or "tian kan." The below four characters are the Branch (地支), or "de zi."

Day Master (日元)

The Day Master (日元), or "Ri Yuen," is the day stem. This represents our self element. The strength of this Day Master is the most important part of the chart as it indicates your favorable stars and unfavorable stars.

The structure of BaZi:

Ten Heavenly Stems (十天干) :

甲 (jiǎ)

乙 (yǐ)

丙 (bǐng)

丁 (dīng)

戊 (wù)

己 (jǐ)

庚 (gēng)

辛 (xīn)

壬 (rén)

癸 (guǐ)

Twelve Earthly Branches (十二地支) :

子 (zǐ)

丑 (chǒu)

寅 (yín)

卯 (mǎo)

辰 (chén)

巳 (sì)

午 (wǔ)

未 (wèi)

申 (shēn)

酉 (yǒu)

戌 (xū)

亥 (hài)

There are Ten Heavenly Stems (Fig 2.2) and Twelve Earthly Branches (Fig 2.3). They have either (-)Yin or (+)Yang properties as well as an elemental property of the Five Elements as shown in the table below.

Ten Heavenly Stems

Stem	Status	Element
Jia 甲	(+)Yang	Wood
Yi 乙	(-)Yin	Wood
Bing 丙	(+)Yang	Fire
Ding 丁	(-)Yin	Fire
Wu 戊	(+)Yang	Earth
Ji 己	(-)Yin	Earth
Geng 庚	(+)Yang	Metal
Xin 辛	(-)Yin	Metal
Ren 壬	(+)Yang	Water
Gui 癸	(-)Yin	Water

Fig 2.2

Twelve Earthly Branches

Branch	Status	Element	Associated Animal
Zi 子	(+)Yang	Water	Rat
Chou 丑	(-)Yin	Earth	Ox
Yin 寅	(+)Yang	Wood	Tiger
Mao 卯	(-)Yin	Wood	Rabbit
Chen 辰	(+)Yang	Earth	Dragon
Si 巳	(-)Yin	Fire	Snake
Wu 午	(+)Yang	Fire	Horse
Wei 未	(-)Yin	Earth	Goat
Shen 申	(+)Yang	Metal	Monkey
You 酉	(-)Yin	Metal	Rooster
Xu 戌	(+)Yang	Earth	Dog
Hai 亥	(-)Yin	Water	Pig

Fig 2.3

Analyzing a BaZi Chart

Earlier on, we mentioned the Ten Heavenly Stems and Twelve Earthly Branches characters that make up a BaZi chart. Once we have the chart done, we are now ready to delve deeper into what each of the elements means pertaining to the information about a person.

Ten Heavenly Stems

The Ten Heavenly Stems and the Twelve Earthly Branches are a "must know" if you are to practice BaZi reading. The reason for this is that each of the characters represented by the Heavenly Stems and Earthly Branches allows us to analyze in-depth and gain a better understanding about a person's character, potential, and destiny with the elements that appear on his/her BaZi Chart.

The Heavenly Stem of your day of birth is referred to as the "Day Master." Your Day Master represents your nature, characteristics, behavior, and even your appearance. All the elements that surround it will impact you in either a bad or good way.

Characteristics of Different Day Masters

Jia (甲) – (+)Yang Wood

Jia Wood Day Masters are commonly steady, outspoken, and righteous with strong willpower. The Wood Masters are intelligent and artistic. They also tend to be conservative and reluctant to make changes.

Characteristics

Steady, Strong Willpower, Outspoken, Righteous, Intelligent, Artistic, Morals, Reputation, Responsible, Honorable, Sympathize, Willing to Help Others, Stubborn, Unable to Compromise, Not as Quick-Witted, Unable to Adapt to Changes.

Yi (乙) – (-)Yin Wood

Unlike the Jia Wood people, the Yi Wood people are defined by their flexibility and adaptability. A Yi Wood person has the ability to adapt to changes quickly and is able to avoid trouble by doing so. Sometimes they tend to change their minds quickly and can be difficult to keep up with them.

Characteristics

Sensitive, Quick-Witted, Adaptability, Modest, Meticulous, Flexible, Realistic, Timid, Dependent, Creative.

Bing (丙) – (+)Yang Fire

Bing Fire types are usually generous and open. They can be vibrant, vivacious, gloomy. They can be poor when it comes to expressing their feelings. Bing Fire people are generally sincere, upright, and noble. They are sentimental, charitable, and usually passionate about a cause, a belief, or a principle.

Characteristics

Open, Generous, Warmth, Passion, Enthusiasm, Leadership Qualities, Straightforward, Amiable, Bighearted, Energetic, Enthusiasm, Reckless, Impatient, Self-opinionated, Mood Swings, Conceited.

Ding (丁) – (-)Yin Fire

Ding Fire people are careful and meticulous. Sometimes, they are quite fickle minded. Ding Fire people usually are good leaders or businesspeople because of their detail-oriented, calculative, and sentimental characteristics.

Characteristics

Conservative, Courteous, Passionate, Quiet, Warm, High Tolerance Levels, Attentive, Careful and Cautious, Thoughtful to Their Loved Ones, Protective Attentive to Details.

Wu (戊) – (+)Yang Earth

Wu Earth Day Masters are almost always steady, reliable, and trustworthy. Wu types, however, tend to be too stubborn and inflexible.

Characteristics

Trustworthy, Optimistic, Open-Minded, Steady, Carefree, Strict, Honest, Stability, Slow, Stubborn, Willful, Self-Centered.

Ji (己) – (-)Yin Earth

Ji Earth people are very productive and resourceful. Ji Earth Day Masters are usually kind and are people you can rely on. Ji Earth people are always understanding and able to accept others. Sometime they lack adaptability and are unable to make quick decisions.

Characteristics

Understanding, Versatile, Steady, Kind, Hardworking, Flexible, High Adaptability, Unfocused, Compromise Easily.

Geng (庚) – (+)Yang Metal

Geng Metal represents the axe or sword. They are tough and able to tolerate hardship and withstand difficulties. Geng Metal people value friendship, and they can be great leaders with their strong characters. But sometimes they can be inflexible and too impulsive when making decisions.

Characteristic

Strong, Sharp, Determined, Straightforward, Strong-willed, Enthusiasm, Determination, Cleanliness, Strong Sense of Justice, Chivalrous Heart, Stubborn, Careless

Xin (辛) – (-)Yin Metal

Xin Metal represents Gold. The Xin Day Master usually loves being in the spotlight. Xin Metal people are quite sentimental but can sometimes be annoying due to their craving for attention.

Characteristics

Sensitive, Unique Opinions, Approachable, Helpful, Sharp, Quick, Attractive, Sociable, Self-Respect, Indulge in Vanity, Willful, Stubborn.

Ren (壬) – (+)Yang Water

Ren Water represents water of the sea or river. The Ren Water Day Masters are adaptive, intelligent, and always seem to be on the move. They are, however, often rebellious and dislike being made to settle down.

Characteristics

Enthusiasm, Sociable, Adaptable, Clever, Intelligent, Inspiring Leadership Qualities, Willful, Lazy, Carefree.

Gui (癸) – (-)Yin Water

Gui Water represents rain or stream water. The Gui Water people are introverts and are good at imaginative and creative thinking. The Gui Water people can be very weak when it comes to managing their feelings and may engage too much in negative thinking.

Characteristics

Steady, Peaceful, Diligent, Hardworking, Endurance, Introvert Personality, Cleanliness, Honest, Down to Earth, Nervous, Innocent, Sensitive, Pessimistic, Negative Thoughts.

This page is intended to be blank.

Twelve Earthly Branches

Sign	Animal	Branch	Status	Element
	Rat	Zi 子	(+)Yang	Water
	Ox	Chou 丑	(-)Yin	Earth
	Tiger	Yin 寅	(+)Yang	Wood
	Rabbit	Mao 卯	(-)Yin	Wood
	Dragon	Chen 辰	(+)Yang	Earth
	Snake	Si 巳	(-)Yin	Fire
	Horse	Wu 午	(+)Yang	Fire
	Goat	Wei 未	(-)Yin	Earth
	Monkey	Shen 申	(+)Yang	Metal
	Rooster	You 酉	(-)Yin	Metal
	Dog	Xu 戌	(+)Yang	Earth
	Pig	Hai 亥	(-)Yin	Water

How to Check BaZi

BaZi and Family Members

In your BaZi, your career, love, and family information can be interpreted in the following way:

Hour 時	Day Master 日主	Month 月	Year 年	Ten Years 大運	Current Year 小運
Your Child	Yourself	Parents	Grandparents		
	Spouse				

Fig 3.1

Fig 3.1: You can see in the BaZi (Four Pillar of Destiny) that each of the pillars represents a person or your family members. The BaZi uses the elements to further analyze the relationships between these members in your life. Believe it or not, it is usually able to achieve 80 percent accuracy!

Eight characters and the elements tend to unite as the basis of numerology, or fortune. The five elements is an ancient Chinese concept of a substance. For philosophy, Chinese medicine, and divination, this refers to the five elements: metal, wood, water, fire, earth. That nature consists of five elements with the rise and fall of the five elements, and nature-produced changes not only affect the fate of the people but also make everything in the universe an endless loop.

This page is intended to be blank.

THE CHINESE CALENDAR

Today, the use of the Chinese calendar is relevant for some East Asian holidays, such as the Chinese New Year, the Duan Wu festival, and the Mid-Autumn Festival. In astrology, it is used to choose the most auspicious date for a wedding or the opening of a business.

In China, the traditional calendar is known as the "agricultural calendar" (農曆/农历) while the Gregorian calendar is known as the "common calendar" (公曆/公历), or "yang calendar" (陰曆/阴历). For more than two thousand years, since the time of Emperor Wu of Han, the month containing the winter solstice has almost always been the eleventh month. (This means the new year starts on the second new moon after the winter solstice unless there is an eleventh or twelfth intercalary month, in which case it starts on the third

new moon). The Chinese system of timekeeping is based on the Heavenly Stems and Earthly Branches.

There are Ten Heavenly Stems and Twelve Earthly Branches. They have either yin or yang properties as well as an elemental property of the Five Elements.

The stems combine with the branches in a sequence shown below to form a cycle of sixty combinations known as the "Sixty Jia Zi." Refer to Fig 4.1 for The Sixty Jia Zi Table.

Fig 3.2 - The relationship between the stem of the year and the stem of the month.

Year	Yin 1st month	Mao 2nd month	Chen 3rd month	Si 4th month	Wu 5th month	Wei 6th month	Shen 7th month	You 8th month	Xu 9th month	Hai 10th month	Zi 11th month	Chou 12th month
Jia or Ji	Bing	Ding	Wu	Ji	Geng	Xin	Ren	Gui	Jia	Yi	Bing	Ding
Yi or Geng	Wu	Ji	Geng	Xin	Ren	Gui	Jia	Yi	Bing	Ding	Wu	Ji
Bing or Xin	Geng	Xin	Ren	Gui	Jia	Yi	Bing	Ding	Wu	Ji	Geng	Xin
Ding or Ren	Ren	Gui	Jia	Yi	Bing	Ding	Wu	Ji	Geng	Xin	Ren	Gui
Wu or Gui	Jia	Yi	Bing	Ding	Wu	Ji	Geng	Xin	Ren	Gui	Jia	Yi

Fig 3.3 - The relationship between the stem of the day and the stem of the hour.

Day	Zi hour	Chou hour	Yin hour	Mao hour	Chen hour	Si hour	Wu hour	Wei hour	Shen hour	You hour	Xu hour	Hai hour
Jia or Ji	Jia	Yi	Bing	Ding	Wu	Ji	Geng	Xin	Ren	Gui	Jia	Yi
Yi or Geng	Bing	Ding	Wu	Ji	Geng	Xin	Ren	Gui	Jia	Yi	Bing	Ding
Bing or Xin	Wu	Ji	Geng	Xin	Ren	Gui	Jia	Yi	Bing	Ding	Wu	Ji
Ding or Ren	Geng	Xin	Ren	Gui	Jia	Yi	Bing	Ding	Wu	Ji	Geng	Xin
Wu or Gui	Ren	Gui	Jia	Yi	Bing	Ding	Wu	Ji	Geng	Xin	Ren	Gui

Chinese Lunar-Solar Time and the Hour

In Chinese astrology, BaZi (Four Pillars of Destiny) relies on the comparison of the Chinese Lunar-Solar Time to determine the related hours, day, month, and years for the BaZi chart. Hence, it is a very important step for building a BaZi chart. Without it, or even with the wrong information, it will not be possible to achieve the mission of decoding BaZi.

As the basic guideline for the reader who is keen on reading BaZi as a profession, the basic components of the BaZi of the Ten Heavenly Stem and the Twelve Earthly Branches are important items that one needs to memorize. For both BaZi and feng shui, the Twelve Earthly Branches are used to represent the year, month, day, and hour, whereas the Ten Heavenly Stems are used to represent different elements that you have learned in earlier chapters. The Heavenly Stems and the Earthly Branches are the codes with characteristics representing the

different five elements. It could also be used to represent times, places, directions, animal zodiac signs, and so on.

Plotting BaZi Chart – Year Pillar

The process of plotting a BaZi chart will involve using a Chinese Thousand Year calendar for finding the Day Master. Referring to the Chinese Thousand Year can be hard for beginners. Although the Chinese Thousand Year Calendar is used widely in Asian countries, they are mostly only available in Chinese or Japanese languages. And therefore, I have created an online calculator to help you get started with your BaZi chart.

In your BaZi chart, the months, days, and hours that are used are derived from the Heavenly Stems and the Earthly Branches.

First thing we will need to obtain is the date of birth, hour of birth, and the gender of the person whose BaZi chart we want to plot. This is the essential information required. The date of birth is according to the date as indicated on your birth certificate and not the Lunar Calendar.

For example, we want to plot a BaZi chart of a person born on October 20, 1981. First, we draw a table as follows:

Hour时	Day (Master)日 (主)	Month月	Year年

The pillar for the hour, day, month, and year is based on the combination of Heavenly Stems and Earthly Branches, known as Sixty Jia Zi (甲子). You can infer that the Sixty Jia Zi is made up of tables of different Heavenly Stems and Earthly Branches. Each component runs in sequential order to pair up with one another throughout the sequence, which eventually makes up the entire table.

The Heavenly Stems (十天干) consists of the following:

甲 (**jiǎ**)
乙 (**yǐ**)
丙 (**bǐng**)
丁 (**dīng**)

戊 (wù)

己 (jǐ)

庚 (gēng)

辛 (xīn)

壬 (rén)

癸 (guǐ)

The Earthly Branches (十二地支) consists of the following:

子 (zǐ)

丑 (chǒu)

寅 (yín)

卯 (mǎo)

辰 (chén)

巳 (sì)

午 (wǔ)

未 (wèi)

申 (shēn)

酉 (yǒu)

戌 (xū)

亥 (hài)

Hence, to obtain a pillar of the Sixty Jia Zi, we combine the Heavenly Stems and the Earthly Branches to get the table as shown on Fig 4.1.

The sequence of the Heavenly Stems and Earthly Branches continues to run until it reaches Gui-Hai (癸亥), the sixtieth pillar, and the sequence restarts from the first pillar again. It is called Sixty Jia Zi because it starts from the Jia Zi pillar and it has sixty pillars.

Fig 4.1 The Sixty Jia Zi Table

1	2	3	4	5	6	7	8	9	10	11	12
Jia-Zi	Yi-Chou	Bing-Yin	Ding-Mao	Wu-Chen	Ji-Si	Geng-Wu	Xin-Wei	Ren-Shen	Gui-You	Jia-Xu	Yi-hai
13	14	15	16	17	18	19	20	21	22	23	24
Bing-Zi	Ding-Chou	Wu-Yin	Ji-Mao	Geng-Chen	Xin-Si	Ren-Wu	Gui-Wei	Jia-Shen	Yi-You	Bing-Xu	Ding-Hai
25	26	27	28	29	30	31	32	33	34	35	36
Wu-Zi	Ji-Chou	Geng-Yin	Xin-Mao	Ren-Chen	Gui-Si	Jia-Wu	Yi-Wei	Bing-Shen	Ding-You	Wu-Xu	Ji-Hai
37	38	39	40	41	42	43	44	45	46	47	48
Geng-Zi	Xin-Chou	Ren-Yin	Gui-Mao	Jia-Chen	Yi-Si	Bing-Wu	Ding-Wei	Wu-Shen	Ji-You	Geng-Xu	Xin-Hai
49	50	51	52	53	54	55	56	57	58	59	60
Ren-Zi	Gui-Chou	Jia-Yin	Yi-Mao	Bing-Chen	Ding-Si	Wu-Wu	Ji-Wei	Geng-Shen	Xin-You	Ren-Xu	Gui-Hai

The Time Chart

The time chart for BaZi refers to the different Earthly Branches, which is associated with a different set of timing.

Twelve Earthly Branches (十二地支)
Timing
子（Zi）
23-1
丑（Chou）
1-3
寅（Yin）
3-5
卯（Mao）
5-7
辰（Chen）
7-9
巳（Si）
9-11
午（Wu）
11-13

未（Wei）
13-15
申（Shen）
15-17
酉（You）
17-19
戌（Xu）
19-21
亥（Hai）
21-23

How to Plot a BaZi

To plot the year pillar of the natal chart, we find the Sixty Jia Zi pillar for the year 1981. Using the Chinese Thousand Year Calendar, we find:

1. The year 1981 pillar is 辛酉

2. Month of October is 戊戌

3. Day of the 20th is 辛未

4. Time at 10:00 a.m. is 癸巳.

(Refer to the Stem of the Hour Table to find the first letter, then refer to the Twelve Earthly Branches chart for the second letter.)

Finally, the BaZi chart for birth day on October 20, 1981, at 10:00 a.m. should look like this:

Hour 时	Day (Master)日 (主)	Month 月	Year 年
癸 gui	辛 xin	戊 wu	辛 xin
巳 si	未 wei	戌 xu	酉 you

Refer to the Chinese Thousand Year Calendar to plot a BaZi Chart.

How to Find the Ten Year Luck Cycle

By referring to the month pillar on the individual BaZi chart, you will be able to determine the next ten years cycle on the chart.

This consists of:

> 1. Determining the order
>
> 2. Calculating when the cycle starts based on your birth

The rules are:

Forward-Left-to-Right: Yang Male Day-Master/ Yin Female Day-Master

Reverse-Right-to-Left: Yin Male Day-Master/ Yang Female Day-Master

Heavenly Stems (十天干) :

丁 ding	丙 bing	乙 yi	甲 jia	癸 qui	壬 ren	辛 xin	庚 gen	己 ji	戊 wu
1988	1998	2008	2018	2028	2038	2048	2058	2068	2078

Branches (十二地支) :

酉 you	申 shen	未 wei	午 wu	巳 si	辰 chen	卯 mao	寅 yin	丑 chou	子 zi
1988	1998	2008	2018	2028	2038	2048	2058	2068	2078

1. Use the table below to find the next character element that is next/before your month pillar and write it down by following the rule sequence.

2. To determine when the luck cycle starts, we use the day of birth minus the next Lunar-Solar Calendar season transition day and divide this by three. Then we round up from the results to determine the actual year that the first pillar should start.

For example: October, 20 1981- 10:00 a.m.

October 20 - October 9 = 13 days

13 days / 3 = 4.3. After rounding-up, his luck-cycle starts at four years old.

Strong Master versus Weak Master

As mentioned earlier, the behavior and good elements found for a Strong Day Master work entire differently as a Weak Master. We shall start by applying the Strong or Weak Day Master Season Table to determine its relationship to the BaZi chart.

Often, some practice BaZi by simply referring to the season of the month to determine a Strong or Weak Day Master. But due to the complication of the four pillar structure, the relationship between the rest of the elements within the pillars will also impact the strength of the Day Master. Hence, it is not sufficient to compare the element of the Day Master with the season that one was born in. A more detailed method will be sometimes required for BaZi. You will later notice it requires a lot of practice to be able to judge the complicated BaZi of one person. A good way to

start is to refer to the BaZi software and start building your skills over time.

Visit the following website to generate your BaZi:

http://learnbazi.weebly.com/

Fig 4.2 The Strong or Weak Day Master Season Table

Day / Month	寅 (Yin)	卯 (Mao)	辰 (Chen)	巳 (Si)	午 (Wu)	未 (Wei)	申 (Shen)	酉 (You)	戌 (Xu)	亥 (Hai)	子 (Zi)	丑 (Chou)
甲 (Jia)	Strong	Strong	Strong	Weak	Weak	Weak	Weak	Weak	Weak	Strong	Strong	Strong
乙 (Yi)	Strong	Strong	Strong	Weak	Weak	Weak	Weak	Weak	Weak	Strong	Strong	Strong
丙 (Bing)	Strong	Strong	Strong	Strong	Strong	Strong	Weak	Weak	Weak	Weak	Weak	Weak
丁 (Ding)	Strong	Strong	Strong	Strong	Strong	Strong	Weak	Weak	Weak	Weak	Weak	Weak
戊 (Wu)	Weak	Weak	Weak	Strong	Strong	Strong	Weak	Weak	Weak	Weak	Weak	Weak
己 (Ji)	Weak	Weak	Weak	Strong	Strong	Strong	Weak	Weak	Weak	Weak	Weak	Weak
庚 (Geng)	Weak	Weak	Weak	Weak	Weak	Weak	Strong	Strong	Strong	Weak	Weak	Weak
辛 (Xin)	Weak	Weak	Weak	Weak	Weak	Weak	Strong	Strong	Strong	Weak	Weak	Weak
壬 (Ren)	Weak	Weak	Weak	Weak	Weak	Weak	Strong	Strong	Strong	Strong	Strong	Strong
癸 (Gui)	Weak	Weak	Weak	Weak	Weak	Weak	Strong	Strong	Strong	Strong	Strong	Strong

Using the Strong or Weak Day Master to Determine One's Favor Elements

Once you have found out the sign of the Day Master, the next step will allow you to find out the favor elements that will strengthen or weaken a Day Master. It is important because it will allow you to realize the quality of a person's BaZi and his/her information.

Strong Day Master

- Likes – Wealth Element/Seven Killings/Eating God

- Dislikes – Resource Element/Friend Element

Weak Day Master

- Likes – Resource Element/Friend Element
- Dislikes – Wealth Elements/Seven Killings/Eating God

Moving on to the next chapter, we will discuss the characteristics of the elements in a BaZi on Ten Gods to help you understand the different ways it behaves for a Strong or Weak Day Master.

THE TEN GOD

The Ten Gods, sometimes known as Ten Deities, is the representative of an element that appears in the BaZi. The information is technically information derived from the birth date/hour/month/year of a person. To determine a Ten God in a BaZi is not as hard as interpreting them. The Ten Gods Details section below makes it easy for you to reference. Please also note that the term "Gods" is just a name; it is statistical in nature and does not represent anything religious. The naming of the BaZi elements sometimes can be misleading or confusing, but it generally is only

meant for identification purposes.

Different people may have a different understanding of the wording, so the translations can sometimes be very confusing. The translated terms should not influence the perception of the readers and students.

The Ten God Table

Ten God Details

The Direct Star (正官)

In the male BaZi, it represents his son.

For a female BaZi, it represents her husband.

Characteristics of the Direct Officer

The Direct Officer represents status, rank, reputation, ethics and law, discipline, order, regulations, rules and so on. Direct officer also means that the attitude of management capabilities and constraints can force open behavior, noble reputation, outstanding credit, elegance, and dignified and candid manners.

Advantages of the Direct Star

When the Direct Star is not being destroyed by any element in a person's BaZi, the person will be able to exhibit its advantage such as upright, honorable, kindhearted, polite, law-abiding, enthusiastic service, rational, and self-discipline. Leadership can win the respect of others.

Disadvantages of the Direct Star

When the Direct Star itself is strong or has destroyed the harmony of the BaZi, it will exhibit a shortcoming such as inflexible, stiff, rigid, cautious, legalistic, , always worried about everything, does not trust, and indecisive. They often miss good opportunities in their life.

Suitable for Industry

Best to engage in politics, public officials, government agencies, legal, judicial, company executives and so on with the nature of the administration or management of the industry.

The Seven Killing Officer (偏官）

For a male, it represents his daughter. For female BaZi, the appearance of it represents her lover.

Characteristics of the Seven Killing Star

The Seven Killing Star represents authority, rebel forces, extreme and adventurous, courageous and brave. But also self-willed, , wanton, fiery impatience, arbitrary, adventurous,. It also represents lack of consideration, which often results in loneliness and helpless situations.

Advantages of the Seven Killing Star

When the Direct Star is not being destroyed by any element in a person's BaZi, the person will be able to exhibit its advantages, such as courage, good intuitive judgment, high-spirited, and able to overcome difficult challenges with their revolutionary spirit and rebellious character. Most with the good Seven Killing Star have excellent talents in governing, making them great leaders.

Disadvantages the Seven Killing Star

When the Direct Star itself is strong or has destroyed the harmony of the BaZi, it will exhibit a shortcoming, such as extreme rebellion, and bring troubles. It will make a person feel lonely and helpless, revengeful, and often dissatisfied with the reality of situations, with many ups and downs in their career path. The Seven Killing Star will usually act impulsively or recklessly, which is suitable for engaging in demanding work.

Suitable for Industry

Best engage in military, police, athletes, surgeons, marketing director, reporter, detective, and other difficult and highly challenging work.

The Direct Resource Star (正印)

Direct Resource Star is the kind star. It represents the mother of a male or female BaZi.

Characteristics of the Direct Resource Star

Direct Resource Star represents the credibility and knowledge, which implies power. It is a symbol of good qualification, gentle, elegant, kind, attention to spiritual life, outgoing and also good luck, longevity, and prosperity.

If a Direct Star appears on the same column or is a close neighbor in a person's BaZi, the positive will be strengthened and become more apparent.

Advantages of the Direct Resource Star

When the Direct Star is not being destroyed by any element in a person's BaZi, the person will be able to exhibit its advantage, such as being smart, elegant, kind, and attain learning to enrich themselves. They are usually people who are elegant, able to self-motivate, with a noble character, enjoy pursuing new knowledge and gaining people's trust in them.

Disadvantages of the Direct Resource Star

When the Direct Star itself is strong or has destroyed the harmony of the BaZi, it will exhibit the shortcoming, such as too dependent, develop lazy habits, always reluctant to themselves, easily detached from reality.

Suitable for Industry

Should be engaged in cultural, educational, academic, religious, charitable, and other industries that have need of love and care.

Indirect Resource Star (偏印)

Indirect Resource Star can be considered as the stepmother for both male and female. If there is no Direct Resource Star found in a person's BaZi, it can then be referred to as the mother.

Characteristics of the Indirect Resource Star

Indirect Resource Star represents talent and knowledge. Although its nature is different from the Direct Resource Star, the Indirect Resource Star has an excellent ability to comprehend thinking but in a rather unusual approach. They like fantasy and have creativity, design, and planning talent. They do not practice in the general way of thinking. Their unique form of new ideas and creativity are engaged in research work, and, therefore, the Indirect Resource Star is a symbol of creativity.

The Indirect Resource Star people usually are attached to fantasy and have a shortcoming of not being realistic. They do not enjoy being sociable or with a crowd, and they can be indecisive and often in a dilemma.

Advantages of the Indirect Resource Star

When the Direct Star is not being destroyed by any element in a person's BaZi, the person will be able to exhibit its advantage, such as thinking delicately, witty, sensitive, high morals, insightful, and creative. They are superb in unique thinking and are able to approach things with different techniques. But often feel insecure. They have a unique form of thinking, which makes them good at development of new planning and design, and are creative with products, technology, or methods.

Disadvantages of the Indirect Resource Star

When the Direct Star itself is strong or has destroyed the harmony of the BaZi, it will exhibit the shortcoming, such as paranoid, extraordinarily weird, living alone or having a poor community life, as they do not like to socialize. They lack patience. Self-centered and like to ignore the opinions of others.

Suitable for Industry

Best to engage in specialized or professional aspects. An occupation that could highlight individual performance, such as research, invention, design, creation, science and technology, martial arts, performing arts, marketing, direct marketing, advertising, models, porn stars and other special industries.

Direct Wealth Star (正財)

Direct Wealth Star represents a wife in a male BaZi. In a female BaZi or for a male who does not have an Indirect Wealth Star, it represents a father.

Characteristics of the Direct Wealth Star

The Direct Wealth Star represents uprightness, righteousness, and hard work. Therefore it is a symbol of prudent fiscal integrity. The Direct Wealth Star can distinguish clearly between right and wrong, diligence and frugality. They are endowed with the gift of good financial management skills and usually are able to accumulate wealth.

If there is a "Food God" located next to or close neighbors with the Direct Wealth star, the positive power will be strengthened to make them become rich.

Advantages of the Direct Wealth Star

When the Direct Star is not being destroyed by any element in a person's BaZi, the person will be able to exhibit its advantage, such as hard-working, upright, and righteous, and they usually have strong family values. They have good economic concepts to make them good executives.

Disadvantages of the Direct Wealth Star

When the Direct Star itself is strong or has destroyed the harmony of the BaZi, it will exhibit the shortcoming, such as turning into a miser. They can be ruthless to friends and relatives, especially to those who need help and support. They lack the courage to pursue change or unable to break through in life.

Suitable for Industry

Best to engage in sectors such as finance, financial, business, store, shop, accounting, and financial management.

Indirect Wealth Officer (偏財)

Indirect Wealth Officer star represents the father for the BaZis of both men and women. For a male BaZi, it can also sometimes represent their lovers.

Characteristics of the Indirect Wealth Officer Star

Indirect Wealth Officer star represents heroic and generous, capable, fame and fortune, helpful and romantic. People with this star usually gain popularity easily, especially the female, and are very sociable, have good financial know-how and vitality to overcome problems that come to their lives.

Advantages of the Indirect Wealth Officer Star

When the Direct Star is not being destroyed by any element in a person's BaZi, the person will be able to exhibit its advantage, such as able to create opportunities for themselves, able to seize the opportunity to earn money, or manage to get things done neat and quickly and without being dragged.

They have great energy, business acumen, quick wit, generosity, and are passionate, courageous, optimistic, and enterprising, and are not afraid of setbacks.

Disadvantages of the Indirect Wealth Officer Star

When the Direct Star itself is strong or has destroyed the harmony of the BaZi, it will exhibit the shortcoming, such as being too generous, lack of financial management sense, wasteful, extravagant spending. For male or female, it can sometimes represent too many affairs that affect their marriage.

Suitable for Industry

Best to engage in commercial activities, such as business, trade, factories, investment, stocks, securities, and other high-risk activities.

The Cooking God Star (食神)

The Cooking God star is the star of passion. In a female BaZi, it represents her daughter. To a male BaZi, it represents the peace and inactive.

Characteristics of the Cooking God

The Cooking God represents a person's hidden talent, conservative, cheerful, stable life, smart, and self-sufficient.

Advantages of the Cooking God

When the Direct Star is not being destroyed by any element in a person's BaZi, the person will be able to exhibit its advantage, such as cheerful, clever, delicate, focusing on the lifestyle, emotional, and good prosperity.

The Disadvantages of the Cooking God

When the Direct Star itself is strong or has destroyed the harmony of the BaZi, it will exhibit the shortcoming, such as pretentiousness, emptiness, and sometimes unable to vent their inner feelings.

Suitable for Industry

Best to engage in industries such as services, diplomacy, public relations, business, hospitality, teaching, and technology.

The Injured Officer Star (傷官）

The Injured Officer is a Talent Star, which represents the son in a female BaZi. For a male BaZi, it represents the abilities.

Characteristics of the Injured Officer

The Injured Officer represents that a person has outstanding talent, business sense, smart, and intelligent.

Advantages of the Injured Officer

When the Direct Star is not being destroyed by any element in a person's BaZi, the person will be able to exhibit its advantage, such as talent, versatile, appearance, and intellectual, clever, able to create wealth, lofty ideals, desire, ambition, and leadership.

Disadvantages of the Injured officer

When the Direct Star itself is strong or has destroyed the harmony of the BaZi, it will exhibit the shortcoming, such as self-centered, ruthless, stubborn, and unable to accept others' advice. They tend to be unfocused and often make things beyond their ability, which leads to failure.

Suitable for Industry

Best to engage in the industry of literature, art, philosophy, attentive, and sentimental industries, such as artists, musicians, writers, performing arts, script writing.

The Friend Star (比肩)

The Friend Star represents siblings or friends for the BaZis of both males and females.

Characteristics of the Friend Star

The Friend Star stands for "Shoulder" in Chinese, which means equal status, friendship, self-awareness, and self-esteem. With strong self-awareness and self-esteem, one is always eager to keep pace with others.

Advantages of the Friend Star

When the Direct Star is not being destroyed by any element in a person's BaZi, the person will be able to exhibit its advantage, such as optimism, perseverance, independent self-centred and strong-willed. Self-confident and able to stick to their posts and work hard to achieve their goals.

Disadvantages of the Friend Star

When the Direct Star itself is strong or has destroyed the harmony of the BaZi, it will exhibit the shortcoming, such as self-consciousness, arrogant, stubborn, conflict, unable to get along with family members, unable to obey the guidance of the supervisor. Women who do things arbitrarily will sometimes have problems in their love relationship.

Suitable for Industry

Best to be engaged in partnerships, lawyers, accountants, politicians, family business, and negotiations.

The Robbing Star (劫財)

The Robbing Star represents the younger sibling to the BaZi of males and females.

Characteristics of the Robbing Star

A Robbing Star often hides the true colors and has the potential of a self-centered character and possesses a deceiving appearance. It is difficult to understand the complexity of their personality.

Robbing often has strong jealousy, never admits defeat, has ambition, and is bold.

Advantages of the Robbing Star

When the Direct Star is not being destroyed by any element in a person's BaZi, the person will be able to exhibit its advantage, such as often prominent and has a unique character of their own style. In life, they easily make friends, and also easily lose friends.

Disadvantages of the Robbing Star

When the Direct Star itself is strong or has destroyed the harmony of the BaZi, it will exhibit the shortcoming, such as dual personality (both the yin and yang nature), the heart is often self-contradictory, self-conflict. They are temperamental and are often volatile and sometimes jealous of others' success.

Suitable for Industry

Best to engaged in the aspect of leadership, decision making, wholesale chain, government officials, highly competitive area, and business executives.

COMBINATION & CLASH

Five Elements Interactions

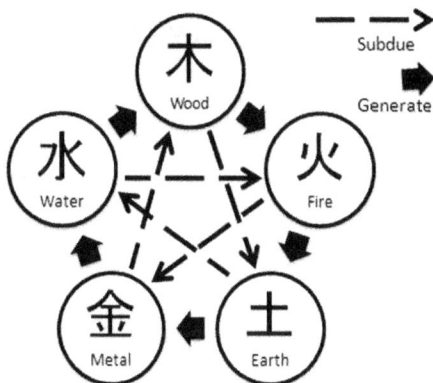

Fig 5.1

Combination & Clash

In the BaZi, there are some special circumstances that might cause the elements to change their nature. The term is known as combinations and crashes, which indicate when they attract or repel between two Heavenly Stems or two Earthly Branches met within a BaZi chart.

Below are some of the rules to be observed when analyzing a BaZi chart. These combinations indicate a powerful network or special relationships. When such a combination occurs in a BaZi chart, it will become the element favorable or unfavorable to the Day Master.

Three Harmony Combinations			
Water Structure	Shen Monkey	Zi Rat	Chen Dragon
Wood Structure	Hai Pig	Mao Rabbit	Wei Goat
Fire Structure	Yin Tiger	Wu Horse	Xu Dog
Metal Structure	Si Snake	You Rooster	Chou Ox

Fig 5.2

The Three Harmony Combinations will turn into powerful elements when a special structure of elements are combined. The Directional Combination is similar to Three Harmony Combination that represent the Earthly Branches in season in a BaZi chart. Note that not all circumstances will result to a combination.

Directional Combinations			
Spring	Yin Tiger (February)	Mao Rabbit (March)	Chen Dragon (April)
Summer	Si Snake (May)	Wu Horse (June)	Wei Goat (July)
Autumn	Shen Monkev (August)	You Rooster (September)	Xu Dog (October)
Winter	Hai Pig (November)	Zi Rat (December)	Chou Ox (January)

Fig 5.3

Six Harmony Combinations			
Zi Rat	+	Chou Ox	= Earth
Yin Tiger	+	Hai Pig	= Wood
Mao Rabbit	+	Xu Dog	= Fire
Chen Dragon	+	You Rooster	= Metal
Si Snake	+	Shen Monkey	= Water
Wei Goat	+	Wu Horse	= Fire

Fig 5.4

The Six Harmony Combinations often occur when a Day Master meets a certain ten-year cycle or during a particular year. This is why we sometimes hear there is good or bad year for a certain horoscope.

Clashes in BaZi

A Clash in a BaZi occurs when two repelling elements meet. A clash in a BaZi represents obstacles and hardship for the Day Master. Depending on the type of clash, a person can experience difficulties in relationships, lose someone, or even encounter accidents and illness. Note that not all present elements might be a clash if it appears in the one person's BaZi. The relevant elements will have to be next to each other to be effective.

Clashes Relationships

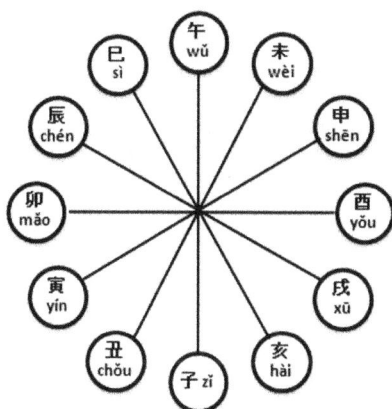

Fig 5.5

Six Clashes

Rat	≠	Horse
Ox	≠	Goat
Tiger	≠	Monkey
Rabbit	≠	Rooster
Dragon	≠	Dog
Snake	≠	Pig

Fig 5.6

CASE STUDY

Case Study and Ta Yun

An example of one famous Hong Kong-born movie

star/director's BaZi Four Pillars of Destiny and his

Ta Yun.

He was born April 7, 1954, is a Hong Kong movie star, stuntman, actor, and director.

His BaZi Four Pillars of Destiny is quite unique, and he was ranked number one in the 2010 Chinese Rich & Famous list, published by Forbes (Chinese) magazine. He has a high celebrity income and enjoys a very successful career.

We will leave the Hour Pillar blank because we do not have the information.

Let's see the information given about his wealth luck. (Chart 1. His BaZi table.)

Based on the Strong and Weak Master chart, we can see that he has a Weak Day Master. For Weak Day Master, "Rob wealth" Jie-cai (劫) and "Friends" Bi-jian (比) are his money stars.

Note that a person might not born to be rich. But he/she will still stand a good chance when the opportunity and time is right for them. In his unique BaZi formation, his wealth elements appeared on his chart. He will be very rich between his ten-years cycle of 1993–2003.

Chart 1. His BaZi Chart

Hour时	Day (Master)日 (主)	Month月	Year年
	癸 (guǐ)	戊 (wù) 正官 (官) Direct officer	甲 (jiǎ) 伤官 (伤) Hurting officer
	巳 (sì) 正财 (财) Direct wealth 正官 (官) Direct officer 正印 (印) Direct Resource	辰 (chén) 正官 (官) Direct officer 食神 (食) Food god 比肩 (比) Friends	午 (wǔ) 偏财 (才) Indirect wealth 七杀 (杀) 7 killings

His ten years luck cycles (Ta Yun):

- From his first ten years luck (1963), it shows that he did not have early high education.

- The following ten years luck (1973), with his fame and recognition stars dominating, he became internationally famous. He enjoyed a successful career.

- The third ten years luck (1983) shows strong money stars.

- The fourth ten years luck (1993) shows his original stars, with combination and transformation into money stars, resulted in him still having the good luck of making lots of money.

The fifth ten years luck (2003) shows his money luck is still very strong.

Ten years luck cycle

1963	1973	1983	1993	2003
己 jǐ	庚 gēng	辛 xīn	壬 rén	癸 guǐ
七杀 (杀) 7 killings	正印 (印) Direct Resource	偏印 (卩) Indirect Resource	劫财 (劫) Rob wealth	比肩 (比) Friends
巳 sì	午 wǔ	未 wèi	申 shēn	酉 yǒu
正财 (财) Direct wealth	偏财 (才) Indirect wealth	七杀 (杀) 7 killings	七杀 (杀) 7 killings	偏印 (卩) Indirect Resource
正官 (官) Direct officer	七杀 (杀) 7 killings	偏财 (才) Indirect wealth	偏财 (才) Indirect wealth	
正印 (印) Direct Resource		食神 (食) Food god	食神 (食) Food god	

REMEDIES

Can I change my luck?

Once you have found out about your BaZi chart, the result could be either satisfying or disappointing. The purpose of understanding your BaZi or destiny is to allow you to know what is the "pre" condition and internal factor of yourself. This could help you to be prepared, though you still have to go through it. But you can minimize the effect or misfortune through using feng shui, hard work, determination, charity work, and prayer.

In the Chinese beliefs, our life is influenced by the following main five factors:

"一命二运三风水，四积功德五读书"

• Destiny

Destiny and Luck cannot be changed. Our destiny code can help us to assess the "Strength" and "Weakness" of this natural born good or bad elements we have. By knowing our destiny, we can prepare and then try to adapt to circumstances accordingly.

• Luck

In order to achieve success, we not only require a good life destiny, we also need good luck. Everyone will need to have a smooth ride during our journeys in health, career, wealth, and relationships. In Chinese and Japanese, the word for luck is 運 (wun). 運 can be good or bad. But 運 is customarily followed by another word, 気 (qi), which means energy or air. The Master of Tao once said that when a person is able to 運気 (control your energy), they will be able to attract good luck or good fortune. This is similar to the belief that when one

has the positive energy, they will attract positive energy and become strong. As long as you adopt the right attitude and always try your best, you will be able to create the causes and conditions for your life.

• Feng Shui

Feng shui is about environment conditions that will influence one person. Create the best environment to suit yourself, because when our luck is down, feng shui can help to reduce the effect of bad things and enhance the effects for a better life.

• Charity

Be kind and charitable. If you can make contributions to the society, you generate good cause and effect known as "karma."

• Education

Education opens the door to many opportunities for a better life and future, and it helps us become better people.

References:

http://en.wikipedia.org/wiki/Chinese_cal
endar
http://en.wikipedia.org/wiki/Luck
http://en.wikipedia.org/wiki/Fortune_tel
ling
From Wikipedia, the free encyclopedia

www.ingramcontent.com/pod-product-compliance
Lightning Source LLC
Chambersburg PA
CBHW070959040426
42443CB00007B/579